for the love of ASSH⬤LES

Another Book About Assholes

Archimedes' Printing Shoppe
& Sundry Goodes

for the love of
ASSH⬤LES
Another Book About Assholes

S.J. Russell & Erica Brown
illustrated by Maggie McMahon

By S.J. Russell and Erica Brown
Illustrations by Maggie McMahon
Photography by Peggy Jackson & Erica Brown
Edited by Lucy Noland

Design by A Little Graphix | Titles and text in Good Dog and Chandler 42

Heartfelt thanks to our editors and proof readers, Susan Palmer Marshall and Margaret
Jackson, and our go-to's for all things Scottish: Sandy Marshall and Kerry MacKenzie.

Library of Congress Cataloging-in-Publication Data

Names: Russell, S. J., author. | Brown, Erica Newell, author. | McMahon, Maggie Kathleen, illustration.
Title: For the love of assholes / S. J. Russell and Erica Brown ; illustrated by Maggie McMahon.
Description: Philadelphia, PA: Archimedes' Printing Shoppe & Sundry Goodes LLC, 2021.
Identifiers: LCCN: 2021938110 | Hardcover ISBN: 978-0-9962994-7-3 | Softcover ISBN: 978-1-955517-01-0
Subjects: LCSH Pigs—Fiction. | Roosters—Fiction. | Dogs—Fiction. | Domestic animals—Fiction. |
Farm life—Fiction. | Animal rescue—Fiction. | BISAC FICTION / Animals
Classification: LCC PS3618.U7675 A88 2020 | DDC 813.6--dc23

Printed on Forest Stewardship Council-certified and Sustainable Forest Initiative-certified
paper stock. Proudly made in Pennsauken, New Jersey, USA.

In loving memory of Barbi Q and Gidget

for the love of ASSHOLES

Another Book About Assholes

Raphael **PACKED** his bag.

Since he had no belongings,
this took no time.

Wilbur yawned,
   looked the rooster
      up and down and

plopped himself

    on the straw.

He then burped.

"I won't miss you," said Wilbur.

"I won't miss you," replied Raphael.

"You're such an asshole," said the pig.

"I know," replied the rooster. "But you're a bigger asshole."

"I know."

They looked at each other long and hard.

It was a sobering moment.

2

Wilbur finally looked away.

Then he took a corncob from his slop bucket and whipped it at Raphael's head, knocking the bird to the ground.

Raphael flapped his wings, flew straight at the pig and pecked hard at Wilbur's head.

They sat there concussed.

Wilbur managed to stand.

"So you're going up the road?"

"Yup."

"She put you on craigslist?"

"Yup."

Wilbur shook his head.

Blood from the deep wound dribbled down his face and onto the straw.

ASSHOLE FOR SALE (NJ)

They both turned their attention to the woman who had appeared from the barn.

Armed with her protective stick, she entered the paddock.

They both stared at her.

"OK, Raphael. Let's get you ready," she said.

"This is probably your last chance," Wilbur whispered.

"Yeah, I know," replied Raphael wistfully.

He would miss this.

Raphael flew at the woman's shins, pecking hard.

"I CAN'T WAIT 'TIL YOU'RE GONE!!"

#%$*@!!

she yelled.

The woman stormed out of the paddock as Raphael and
Wilbur laughed and laughed.

And then laughed some more.

"I won't miss you."

"I won't miss you, either."

Not long after, the woman, now sporting soccer shin guards and carrying her stick, returned with another woman.

Raphael greeted the visitor warmly. He even made a flirtatious clucking sound.

Wilbur scratched his head. So did the woman.

Was Raphael smiling?

"Make no mistake," said the woman to the visitor. "He's an asshole."

"Oh, but he seems so sweet."

The **visitor** scooped Raphael under her arm and scratched beneath his wing.

Raphael glanced at Wilbur, then offered up his other wing.

"Look how sweet he is! You're such a good boy, aren't you? Yes, you are. Yes, you are."

Raphael nestled into the visitor's arms and gazed into her eyes.

Wilbur rolled his.

"What the f**k?" muttered the woman in disbelief, massaging her shin.

And off went Raphael to the farm up the road.

"Guess we won't be able to have fart competitions anymore," mumbled Wilbur.

He lumbered back to his enclosure, ignoring the woman.

Was he sad? He could not tell.

But he was something.

The woman grabbed her basket to gather some eggs.

As she neared the coop in Wilbur's paddock, she saw
four chickens chasing the new, scrawny chicken that
she had recently rescued.

Peck, peck, peck, peck, peck . . .

The mean chickens had pecked every feather off the
new chicken's head and were working on her last tail
feathers when the woman shooed them away.

"Oh dear! Come here, Barbi."

The scrawny bald bird,
shell-shocked, was not listening.

"Come here, Barbi," the woman repeated.

"BARBI Q COME HERE!"

But the chicken was too confused.

So the woman picked her up and set
her down outside of the coop.

And inside Wilbur's enclosure.

The woman scattered handfuls of feed.

She lifted the henhouse lid. There were ten eggs.

How she loved fresh eggs.

Then, she heard a soft sound; something moved in the grass. Followed by the faintest Scottish folk melody, which suddenly stopped.

She looked around suspiciously, then gently placed the eggs in her basket. "I can't wait to make a quiche."

Again, she heard the faint sound.

The woman looked around.

But only saw Wilbur, staring intently at the basket.

Then at her face. Then at the basket.

And then at her face.

Barbi Q ambled around the paddock, eyes glazed.

But that wasn't the noise.

There it was again.

"You hear that?" the woman said to no one in particular.

Someone was watching her. And not just Wilbur.

She grabbed her basket and closed the coop door.

For days, James MacNathair—an oversized garden snake who went by "Big Jimmy"— had been

slithering

along in search of something to eat.

His doctor told him to cut it out with the eggs.

But so deep was his love of eating the unborn, he simply could not stop.

"Oh eggs, och aye! The smell of the bonnie wee eggs," he sang as he flicked his forked tongue and slithered toward the coop.

All he knew was he had found the
mother lode.

He could not believe his luck.

And that he was where he
was. Wherever that was.

But his luck soon ran out when he got snagged in the net surrounding the coop.

"Sh*te," escaped his lips. Something was making off with the egg smell.

He stared hard, for what it was worth, his eyesight being awful and all. His tongue flicked in and out.

"Sh*te, sh*te, sh*te," he repeated. "Whar the hell are ma eggs gaun tae the noo?!"

The woman's basket brimmed with eggs.

She joyfully whistled as she walked past Wilbur,
licking her lips and thinking of the magical omelet
she would make.

Wilbur smacked the basket to the ground.

The contents splattered. Wilbur dug in.

Nom. Nom. Nom. Nom. Nom.

"Really, Wilbur?!" said the woman, shaking her head.
"Really?!"

She couldn't stop saying "Really?"

Wilbur kept eating.

"Really???!!!" She angrily wiped the egg splatter
from her shin guards.

The woman then screamed at the sky. Because it was there. And the fluffy clouds had formed an omelet.

She stormed out of the paddock.

Barbi Q watched in horror as Wilbur devoured the eggs.

One of which was hers. She fainted.

Intoxicated by the explosive, heady yolk smell that had suddenly engulfed him, Big Jimmy writhed and wriggled 'til he broke free of the damn netting.

He flicked his tongue. "Thar's definitely eggs o'er thar, pure barry!"

So he slithered eggward, happily singing, "Ooh eggss, eggss . . . och aye!"

Meanwhile . . .

Wilbur had just finished the tenth and final egg.
He was stuffed, his snout covered in yolk.

Wilbur waddled back to his enclosure where Barbi Q
had passed out.

He passed out too. And farted the biggest fart.

Barbi Q revived into a sulfurous cloud.

She couldn't move; her leg was stuck under the pig.

"Could this day get any worse?" she asked in disbelief.

"Get off my leg, you asshole!!"

Wilbur grunted and rolled over onto the chicken.

She was trapped.

The day indeed got worse.

Summoning what was left of her strength, Barbi Q
smashed her beak into Wilbur's butt.

Meanwhile . . .

Big Jimmy wiggled along. He came upon eggshells,
but no eggs.

But there it was again. The smell of eggs.

He picked up his slither.

Big Jimmy slipped into the enclosure.

And bumped into the biggest, hairiest egg he had ever smelled.

Because he really couldn't see. He's a damn snake.

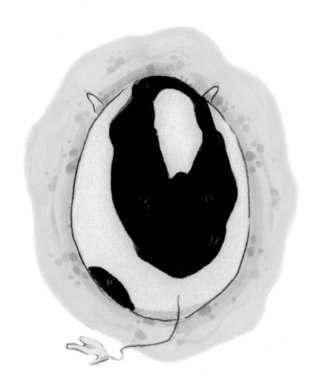

He sidled up to Wilbur's snoring snout.

The egg had air coming out of it. But Big Jimmy didn't care.

It was an egg.

He attempted to swallow it whole.

Comatose, Wilbur dreamed of Raphael.

The dumb rooster was wrestling with him in the paddock, and smothering him with a bale of straw.

In his dream, he couldn't breathe.

And, then, he just couldn't breathe.

Plus, something sharp was sticking in his butt.

Wilbur opened his eyes.

He couldn't believe it. Two other eyes. Right there.

Really big weird ones. Real close-up like.

And they were attached to whatever was covering his snout.

Wilbur jumped up and shook his head. Freed, Barbi Q sucked air back into her lungs.

"Whah, noo," screamed Big Jimmy, as he flew off the hairy egg and sailed across the enclosure. "Keep the heid, Big Jimmy. Keep the heid!"

He looked all peely-wally.

"What the hell are you doing, man?!" Wilbur screamed
at the snake.

"Jings! That egg talkin' tae me??" Big Jimmy muttered.

Wide-eyed, Barbi Q stared at the snake. She hated snakes.

But, she was still alive. Thanks to . . . a snake??

Turning to Wilbur, she screamed, "You jerk!!! You almost killed me!

Big Jimmy felt angry vibrations.

He must have gotten in the middle of something between the hairy egg and whatever was screaming.

He picked a direction he thought was the hell out of there and began slithering.

It was so loud, Gidget, the rescued dog sleeping in the woman's barn, woke up from her favorite dream of sandwiches filled with juicy chicken.

Gidget hated arguments.

She hated pigs.

She hated live chickens.

She hated most people.

She just wanted the woman.
And a big pile of poop
in which to joyously roll.

Was that so wrong?

So she barked and barked.

And barked and barked and barked.

And then she barked some more.

"What's wrong, Gidget?" the woman exclaimed
running into the barn.

Gidget wagged her tail.

"Wanna go for a walk?"

Gidget wagged her tail some more.

Back in the enclosure,
things were not going
well.

"I didn't roll on you,
you stupid, chicken!"
yelled Wilbur, egg on
his face.

"You did too!" Barbi Q
yelled even louder.

Barbi Q pecked Wilbur in the face. Wilbur screamed.

Big Jimmy was still trying to figure out how to get the hell out of the enclosure.

Wilbur plucked one of Barbi Q's last tail feathers. Barbi Q screamed.

Gidget and the woman ran toward the enclosure.

And arrived just as Big Jimmy was leaving.

"Och aye the noo! Fit's dain!" Big Jimmy greeted the two figures.

"It's a snake. It's a snake. It's a huge f**king snake! I hate snakes!!!" the woman screamed.

But Gidget loved snakes. Soft in the middle and chewy, wiggly and long. Gleefully, she grabbed Big Jimmy and swung him round and round.

"Ah'm gaun tae boooooooke," warned Big Jimmy.

Wilbur and Barbi Q stared at the whirlygig that was now Big Jimmy.

"He is the only reason I will live to lay another egg," she thought.

Big Jimmy grew queasier as the trees, clouds and grass blurred, "Oh boy, oh boy, oh boy."

Barbi Q could stand it no longer.

She ran toward the dog and pecked Gidget's paws.

"Stop it you asshole!" Barbi Q screamed.

Gidget licked her lips, envisioning the chicken in a sandwich.

She lost her grip on Big Jimmy, catapulting him away from the enclosure where he landed with a THUNK.

"Arsehole eggss. Yer aff yer heids, all o' ye. I'm sae done with eggss."

Gidget grabbed Barbi Q's last tail feather. And out it came.

"Gidget, noooooo!!!" The woman was fast. But not fast enough.

"Noooooooooooo!!!" cried the chicken, grabbing her butt.

The woman seized Gidget's collar, and steered her back to the barn.

"Raphael, you don't know what you're missing," reminisced Wilbur.

Time passed. As time does.

The woman felt terrible for the chicken who was now
bald on her head and butt.

So she fashioned a wee wig and a little pair of pants.

And she left Barbi Q with Wilbur, who wasn't quite
as mean as the chickens.

"You like to fart?" offered Wilbur. He missed Raphael.

And he didn't hate the **stupid** chicken.

"No," Barbi Q replied.

"Wanna see who can fart the loudest?"

"No, I do not."

"Can I have one of your eggs? Ups my fart game."

This made her smile. She knew not why.

"You are such an asshole."

"I know," he winked at her. "But, assholes need love too."

The end.

THE REAL ASSHOLES OF NEW JERSEY

Wilbur

Raphael

Gidget

Big Jimmy

Barbi Q

THE AUTHORS & ILLUSTRATOR

Founder of Diamonds in the Ruff Dog Rescue, a certified dog trainer and talented mixologist, with a master's in Business Admin, Erica Brown has provided and found homes for creatures great and small for many, many years, including all of the assholes in this book. She shares her home on eight acres in New Jersey with her many rescued dogs, chickens, and an infamous pig.

For S.J. Russell her love for animals runs deep; she is especially inspired by the ill-mannered and ill-tempered. A writer and attorney, Russell shares her Philly home with a patient spouse and enough cats to solidify her cat lady status as "crazy."

Maggie McMahon is a Philly artist who loves animals 'n sh*t. She shares her home with a rescued pure Phillybred dog from the city's open-intake shelter and has two cats straight off the streets of Philly.

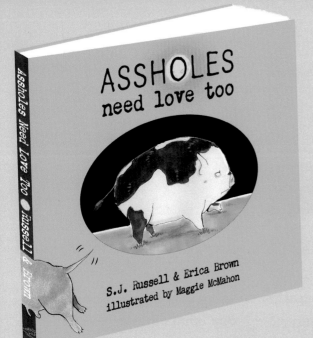

"a warm but wicked can't-we-all-just-get-along ode to the jerks in your life will delight fans of *Go the F**k to Sleep* and *P Is for Pterodactyl.*"
— NYT #1 Bestselling Author, A.J. Finn

"In my long political career, I've known many assholes, some of whom I've even voted for, but the assholes described in this book are by far the most lovable. A must read!"
— Former Governor of Pennsylvania, Ed Rendell

"What if *Charlotte's Web* and *Fight Club* had a baby?
Well, it might be something like *Assholes Need Love Too*; a true(ish) story that proves there's a reward in giving those who most annoy us a chance."
— Steve Morrison, *The Preston and Steve Show* on WMMR

Archimedes' Printing Shoppe & Sundry Goodes

DISCLAIMER: This is a work of mostly nonfiction. In fact, the names, characters and incidences have not been changed one bit: They all refer to the actual assholes in this book. (OK, we might have done the Scottish accent on the snake.) Notwithstanding, any resemblance to any other pigs, roosters, chickens, dogs, snakes, eggs (unborn chickens) or assholes, living or dead, or actual places, events, incidents or businesses is purely coincidental.